MARRIAGE ON PURPOSE

*Saying "I Do" When We
Should Have Said "No Clue!"*

Discussion Guide

DAN SEABORN
DR. PETER NEWHOUSE
ALAN SEABORN

Marriage on Purpose
Discussion Guide

Published by Winning At Home, Zeeland, Michigan, www.winningathome.com.

Acknowledgments

We would like to acknowledge Jeff Kohlinger of Mid-Michigan Community Family Ministries for his role in the development of this discussion guide. His desire and commitment to help marriages grow motivated him to create an outline for this resource, which gave us a great start to create this valuable tool to accompany *Marriage on Purpose*. Thanks Jeff!

We would also like to acknowledge our wives! They deserve a lot of credit for their support and willingness to share personal information about each of our marriages. They all have a genuine desire to help other couples by sharing these stories of our own experiences in an effort to encourage other couples.

Thank you, Jane (Dan), Shawn Maree (Peter), and Annaliese (Alan)!

Table of Contents

Leader's Discussion Notes

Thank you for being willing to lead a group discussion about *Marriage on Purpose*. The following guide has been developed as a tool to help you in leading that discussion.

The guide is essentially a set of suggested discussion questions for each week based on the book. It assumes the participants will have read the applicable chapter(s) of the book ahead of time.

The guide is structured so that you can choose how many sessions you want to tackle each week. We recommend you start with an introductory week where you provide an overview of how the discussion will go each week and have a chance to introduce yourselves to one another. We have included a couple of ice breakers for you to use to help serve that purpose. Ice breakers can still be helpful if a group has been meeting together for a while as it lends itself to asking questions that may have never come up before in conversation. It's also a way to just have fun and relax together. We know couples may have some trepidation in discussing parts of their relationship with other people, especially if they are experiencing some challenges. Helping people get to know one another and trust each other better will help in that process. Be sensitive to that and be open yourself as that will encourage others to be open.

By holding an introductory meeting, you also give everyone a chance to make sure they have the materials they need and to read the chapter(s) you will be discussing at your first official discussion.

Below is a suggested discussion schedule, but of course you may already have your own ideas.

- 10 minutes – Gather/Chat; open in prayer

- 5-10 minutes – Review the prior week's homework and share "Ah-hah" moments or unanswered questions from the prior week

- 30-40 minutes – Work through the discussion questions for that week's session

- 5-15 minutes – Take prayer requests, point out this week's homework, close in prayer

A note about prayer time

It can be helpful to set boundaries for prayer time because prayer in groups can easily take up more time than you realize. This is especially true if people start requesting prayer for people other than themselves. People often find it hard to ask for prayer for themselves or for them as a couple. It makes them vulnerable and sometimes uncomfortable.

Therefore, we encourage you to talk about prayer ahead of time. Explain how it will work and why. Establish that the aim of this discussion group is to help everyone grow in their marriage relationship so it would be helpful to limit prayer requests to be just about the participants in the group and their marriages. This will hopefully help people to focus on why they are there and seek prayer for their relationship. It is always beneficial if leaders show by example.

Ice Breaker Ideas

Ring the Bell Icebreaker

This is a fun introductory icebreaker game for couples, the host or hostess announces that they are going to describe a category and ring a bell when they do so. A couple that matches the description is to raise their hands. Use the following categories or come up with some of your own:

I am looking for the couple who . . .

- Can show me the most pictures of the two of them together.

- Can tell me the funniest real-life wedding or honeymoon story.

- Has birthed the most children between their wedding day and 5th anniversary.

- Married on or closest to an official holiday.

- Married on or closest to one of their birthdays.

- Has the most unique hobby they enjoy doing together.

- Lived the furthest apart when they went out on their first date.

- Looks the most alike (as voted on by everyone).

- Has an interesting or unique first date story.

The Newlywed Game

Pick some or all couples to play the game and have the women leave the room. Ask the men some questions and record their answers. When the women return, ask the women to answer the same questions and see which match. The winning couple has the most matching answers. Use the following questions or choose some of your own:

- What is your wife's favorite song (or movie, flower, book, etc.)?

- The thing I love most about my wife is...

- My wife dislikes my...

- My wife's favorite treat is...

- If your wife could have a new car or new clothes, which would she choose?

- Who said "I love you" first?

- Who is the most patient in the relationship?

- Who is the most stubborn?

- Who is the first to apologize?

- Where did you go on your first date?

- Who is the better cook?

Suggestions for your discussion time

There are a mix of questions designed to get the class talking about the concepts presented in each chapter, and to open up and share about how each of these concepts plays out in their own marriages (particularly stories or examples of success or failure).

The primary benefit of this gathering will depend on the extent that your group members are willing to open up and share from their personal lives through the discussion questions. This will likely take some time as class members develop more familiarity and trust with each other. So, at least for the first couple of weeks, try to be prepared with examples from your own marriage that you can share.

Each week also includes a series of "homework" questions that are designed to help each couple spend 30-60 minutes each week, between meetings, discussing and applying the prior week's material to their marriages. Please be sure to point out this homework each week at the end of the session. If possible, please also try to reserve 5 to 10 minutes at the start of each class to give the couples a chance to share anything they learned or questions from their homework efforts.

If you have only a 60-minute discussion, there are likely more questions than you will be able to cover in the allotted period. So, as leaders, please choose those questions that you think will be most beneficial for your class and focus on those.

Sessions Outline

You may decide to do one session per week or combine a few sessions depending on your available time, but we encourage you to take your time with the material to get the most out of it.

Session 1   Make God Your Top Priority

Session 2   Work on *You*

Session 3   Communication: Listening

Session 4   Communication: Talking

Session 5   Selfishness – Empathy and Love Languages

Session 6   Forgiveness

Session 7   Apologizing

Session 8   Differences

Session 9   Staying Connected

Special notes for specific sessions

Session 2

In this session, we talk about focusing on self. Most questions will ask each spouse to share with the other spouse only opportunities that the person sees in his/her own life for change or improvement, not to point those out for their partner. People may, of course, invite their spouse to share suggestions for changes the other could make, if they like, but this is optional.

Session 4/5

At the end of Session 4, remind participants before they begin Session 5 that a significant part of the Session 5 discussion will include discussing each person's "love languages" from Gary Chapman's book *The 5 Love Languages*. Be sure to point out to participants the part of the homework that asks them to take a short "love languages" online quiz before coming to class on that session, particularly if they do not know what their primary love language is or have never encountered this concept before.

Session 6/7

These sessions involve a discussion of both forgiveness and apologizing. These terms overlap and can sometimes cause confusion, which might happen in your discussion time. One way to look at it is that apologies and forgiveness are two sides of the same coin. We are commanded to forgive whether or not the person who wronged or harmed us apologizes or asks for forgiveness. That is the main point and focus of Session 6. In a healthy relationship, it is also important to genuinely apologize or seek forgiveness when we have hurt or wronged another. That is the main point and focus of Session 7. Often, and always where sin is involved, apologizing and asking for forgiveness are essentially one and the same. But there are also likely situations where one spouse has hurt another where no sin is involved. In that situation, the right and healthy thing to do is apologize for the hurt caused (even if asking for forgiveness is not warranted).

In the context of these two chapters, "forgiveness" focuses on the act of forgiveness on the part of the person who has been wronged, while "apologizing" focuses on the act of apologizing on the part of the person who did or said something to the person hurt or being wronged. Keeping that distinction in mind as you discuss these chapters may be the best way to avoid or help to resolve any confusion that might arise.

Session 8/9

The last two sessions involve how couples approach differences of opinion, on both minor and major matters. As we point out (see pages 129-130), there can be times when we reach irreconcilable differences over matters that are more serious and may require a mentor couple to help us work through the issue or even formal counseling or coaching. Please be sensitive to these realities as you lead discussions on those sessions. If possible, be prepared going into the class with a list of the resources your church makes available to couples struggling with significant irreconcilable differences and others who may benefit from help from a mentor couple or more formal counseling or coaching.

Final thoughts on leading discussion groups

Thank you for coming alongside couples to help them succeed in their marriages. We believe you are leading this group because of the nudge you received from God along with your personal desire to help people have more peace and joy in their marriages so they will better reflect the heart of Jesus.

Don't be discouraged if people don't open up immediately. It takes time. Continue to use ice breakers, examples from your own marriage, the guidance of the Holy Spirit, and prayer to help you break down barriers and get couples to open up. You have obeyed God by gathering the group, encouraging discussion and prayer, and by opening your heart and allowing God to work through it to these couples.

Thank you and God bless you as you lead!

Make God Your Top Priority

KEY THEME

"The most important truth for a married couple is this: if they each keep God their number one priority, he will stabilize and strengthen their marriage during even the hardest times."

Chapter 1 – Make God Your Top Priority

Our Relationship to God and Each Other (pp.13-14).

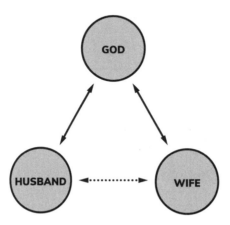

The triangle diagram illustrates our relationship to God and each other.

1. Describe how the diagram works as it relates to our relationship to God and to each other as Husband and Wife.

2. What happens as we each grow closer to God?

3. As we each move further away from God?

4. As one grows closer and one moves further away?

5. How have you seen this dynamic at work in your own marriage?

Praying Together: Inviting God In (pp. 15-17)

Dan says he has encountered "couple after couple who have shared that they don't pray together because it's uncomfortable." (p. 16).

1. Why do you think this statement is true?

2. Have you found that to be true in your marriage? Why or why not?

3. How does prayer help in our relationship with God and with our spouse?

4. Is there something that helped you overcome the initial discomfort of praying together?

Establishing a Purposeful Marriage (pp. 21-23)

We believe two keys to a purposeful marriage are approaching whatever comes your way with *commitment and contentment.*

These verses are helpful in supporting these approaches.

"I know what it is to be in need, and I know what it is to have plenty. I have learned the secret of being content in any and every situation, whether well fed or hungry, whether living in plenty or in want. I can do all this through him who gives me strength." Philippians 4:12-13 (NIV)

1. How are both commitment and contentment essential for a marriage on purpose?

2. In which of these two areas have you had the most success and in which have you struggled the most?

3. Can you share any stories from your marriage that illustrate how these two dynamics play out?

It Starts with You (pp. 23-30)

We believe there are **three "musts"** for a purposeful marriage:

- **Your value and purpose must be found in Christ.**

- **To find your value in Christ you must know who he is.**

- **You must trust God completely.**

In reference to the first "must," instead of trying to get your spouse to help you fix your unhappiness, you need to go find your value and identity in Christ.

1. Why is this so critical?

2. How would you do this?

In reference to the second "must," you are encouraged to spend more "listening time" with God.

1. Why is that important?

2. Why is it often so hard?

3. How (in practical ways) can you make that easier?

In reference to the third "must," we believe God is always at work in your marriage, even when it's painful or you can't see why or how at the time. Even when he doesn't give you what you think you need at the time.

1. Why is trusting God through these situations so hard yet so essential?

2. What is it about God and his character that should give us encouragement to do so?

3. Can anyone share from personal experience how any of these three "musts" have played out in your marriage?

Homework

It's important to find 30 to 60 minutes of uninterrupted time this week to sit down with your spouse and work through the following questions. Pray together at the start and end of your time together, asking God for honesty and grace with each other as you share and for his strength to work on any changes you desire to make.

- Discuss the history of your marriage relationship using the triangle diagram. Where are you now?

- If you are not both moving closer to God, what can each of you do to change that?

- How would you characterize the strength of your prayer life, individually and as a couple?

- Have you prayed together this week? Try to find a consistent time daily, or at least a few days each week, to pray together with your spouse, even if only for a few moments as you start or end the day.

- Share with your spouse where you are on each of the three "musts" for a purposeful marriage. Where are you doing best and where could you use improvement?

Read Chapter 2

Work On You

KEY THEME

"Only after you have worked on you can you effectively work on your marriage and support your spouse in changing what they are *willing* to change in themselves."

Chapter 2 – Work on You

How to Start with You (pp. 34-40)

We suggest three ways to "Start with *You*":

- Have grace for yourself and your spouse.

- Allow God to mold you.

- Commit vertically.

1. Explain each of these three aspects in your own words.

2. How does each one help us take the focus off our spouse and put it onto ourselves?

3. Which of these is hardest and which is easiest for you? Why?

4. How do each of these prepare our hearts to be in a position to lovingly share advice or encouragement around areas of potential growth for our spouse?

"For all have sinned and fall short of the glory of God" Romans 3:23 (NIV)

5. Why is admitting our sinfulness, the fact that we've missed the mark, so hard yet so important in focusing first on our role in the relationship?

6. Do you have an example or story to share of how this has made a difference in your life or marriage?

Don't Expect Easy (pp. 40-45)

What makes focusing on our role in a problem so difficult is that it involves surrender and being willing to be honest about our own shortcomings.

1. Peter suggests a "90/10 Rule" as a way to help us do this. What advantages does that approach bring?

2. Dan refers to the "hula-hoop moment" on page 32 and then again on page 44. How in your marriage are you possibly trying to manipulate or sweet-talk your spouse into changing instead of focusing on allowing God to show you where you can change?

3. Alan suggests that in fragile moments, when we are trying to learn something new, we often feel exposed in some way. When have you felt that way?

Homework

It's important to find 30 to 60 minutes of uninterrupted time this week to sit down with your spouse and work through the following questions. Pray together at the start and end of your time together, asking God for honesty and grace with each other as you share and for his strength to work on any changes you desire to make.

- Choose one area in your relationship where you need to make changes and commit to working on those changes in the coming weeks.

- Share with your spouse where you might struggle with the 90/10 Rule.

Read Chapter 3

NOTE: Following the authors' advice in Chapter 2 about focusing on self, most questions will only ask you to share with your spouse opportunities you see in your life for change or improvement, not for your spouse to point those out in your life or you in theirs. We encourage that latter kind of sharing, but only if your spouse asks or invites you to share suggestions in your discussion.

Communication: Listening

KEY THEME

"When we consider communication in a purposeful marriage, talking is second to listening for this reason: if we don't even understand where our partner is coming from, we can't respond in a way that actually addresses their needs or wants."

Chapter 3 – Communication: Listening

Quick to Listen (pp. 47-49)

"My dear brothers and sisters, take note of this: Everyone should be quick to listen, slow to speak and slow to become angry." James 1:19 (NIV)

1. The authors make the distinction between "hearing" and "listening." How is hearing different from listening?

2. Why is listening so much harder than hearing?

3. Why is listening so much more important than hearing when interacting with our spouse?

Slow to Speak (pp. 49-50)

Usually, we practice being slow to speak only when we're not interested in being involved in a conversation.

1. How does being slow to speak build on being quick to listen?

2. Why is being slow to speak hard for many of us?

3. Is being slow to speak hard or easy for you? Why?

4. Can you share any example of this in your life or marriage?

Slow to Become Angry (pp. 50-54)

When we forget the goal of communication is to understand each other, we start to think it's a competition.

1. How does being both quick to listen and slow to speak help us be slow to become angry?

2. How does practicing these three habits help with the ultimate goal of communication – which is to understand the other person (what they are thinking/feeling and why)?

3. How do our emotions, our selfishness, or our desire to be "right" get in the way?

Practical Tips to Listen Well (pp. 54-59)

There are six action steps you can embrace to improve your listening skills:

- Don't interrupt the person speaking.

- Don't multitask.

- Don't zone out.

- Maintain eye contact with the speaker.

- Focus on content, not delivery.

- Embrace periods of silence.

1. Which of these is an area of strength for you, and which is a struggle or challenge? Why?

2. Can you share an example from your own experience to encourage others in your group?

Homework

It's important to find 30 to 60 minutes of uninterrupted time this week to sit down with your spouse and work through the following questions. Pray together at the start and end of your time together, asking God for honesty and grace with each other as you share and for his strength to work on any changes you desire to make.

- Do you only hear your spouse, or are you also a good listener? How do you know? If you're comfortable with it, ask your spouse for his or her input on this question.

- Peter gives six action steps to improve our listening skills. Share with your spouse where you think you do well and where you need to improve.

Read Chapter 4

Communication: Talking

KEY THEME

"Choosing to be disciplined in how we speak to our spouse takes effort and intentionality."

Chapter 4 - Communication: Talking

Conflict (pp. 61-65)

Many people think of conflict as a purely negative thing, but it is a normal part of a relationship. There are healthy ways to handle confrontational moments and we hope you can spend some time reframing conflict and seeing its value in marriage.

1. Why is conflict both normal and, if handled well, healthy for a marriage?

2. Is dealing with conflict natural or hard for you? Why?

Peter offers several ideas for how to work toward healthy and resolution-focused confrontation:

- Stay on topic.

- Keep it short, and don't be repetitive.

- Stay present and future focused.

- Stay positive and kind.

- Stay affirming, and watch your tone.

- Stay calm, and use your thoughts, not your feeling.

- Stay realistic about the best time to talk.

3. Which of these areas is the hardest for you? Why?

4. Can you share with the group any strategies for managing conflict in a healthy way that have worked well in your marriage or any examples of how you handled conflict well?

Honesty (pp. 65-66)

"Instead, we will speak truth in love, growing in every way more and more like Christ, who is the head of his body, the church." Ephesians 4:15 (NLT)

1. What does honest communication involve?

2. Why is honesty so important when it comes to communicating well with your spouse?

3. Can you share a personal example where communicating honestly or failing to do so either helped or hindered your ability to communicate well with your spouse?

Cutting Out the Negative (pp. 66-68)

We reference the book *Fighting for Your Marriage* by Howard Markman, Scott Stanley, and Susan Blumberg to point out four types of negative patterns that signal real trouble for a relationship: escalation, invalidation, withdrawal and avoidance, and negative interpretations.

1. Which of these four is your most natural "go to" response in moments of frustration and conflict? Why?

2. Can you share with the group any examples of how you have found success in battling this natural tendency?

Kindness (pp. 68-75)

According to recent studies, the ratio of positive interactions needed to counteract a single negative interaction can range from 5:1 to 20:1.

1. Discuss why this is true and the relevance of the frequency vs. the magnitude of the negative and positive interactions.

2. Have you found this to be true in your marriage? Why or why not?

3. Can you share with the group any examples of this dynamic in your marriage, either harmful or helpful?

Homework

It's important to find 30 to 60 minutes of uninterrupted time this week to sit down with your spouse and work through the following questions. Pray together at the start and end of your time together, asking God for honesty and grace with each other as you share and for his strength to work on any changes you desire to make.

- Share with your spouse which of the four areas where couples often get tripped up in being disciplined in their speech (conflict, honesty, cutting out the negative, and kindness) is the most difficult for you. What could you do to change or improve in that area?

- Discuss your approach as a couple to conflict and conflict resolution. Is it generally positive and constructive or not? Which of the suggested seven ideas for helping us to reach healthy conflict resolution are areas where you need to focus in order to improve your approach to conflict resolution?

- Which of the four types of negative patterns that signal trouble for a relationship is your most natural "go to" response in moments of conflict/ frustration? What steps can you take to change that?

- Is there a specific hurtful word each of you would like to see eliminated from your conversations? Share that with your spouse and come up with some ideas of what you can do to change that. Commit this week to increasing the ratio of your positive contributions as compared to your negative withdrawals in your relationship.

Read Chapter 5

Part of the discussion next week will involve you and your spouse's primary "love languages" from Gary Chapman's book *The 5 Love Languages*. If you don't know what your love language is, or if it's been a long time and you want to retake the test, please take the love languages quiz available at the following link before next week's class. It should only take you 5 to 10 minutes. www.5lovelanguages.com/quizzes/

Selfishness

KEY THEME

"We all have natural tendencies toward selfishness; but selfishness damages relationships – especially marriages. Instead, we need to root out selfishness by living an others-oriented life, showing empathy, and showing your spouse love through his or her unique love language."

Chapter 5 - Selfishness

What Is Selfishness? (pp. 77-82)

Most of our ideas and decisions run through a filter before they make it out into the world: *How will this affect me?*

1. What is "selfishness" and what is it not? How does properly understanding selflessness help us to better understand selfishness?

2. Why, in light of our fallen human nature, is selfishness such a natural thing and often so hard to overcome?

3. Does fighting selfishness get easier or harder as we get older? Why?

4. In what way is selfishness damaging to our marriage relationship?

5. Can you share a personal struggle with selfishness and how you battled and overcame it?

6. How does thinking of our spouse as an equally valuable person created in God's image help in our battle with selfishness?

The Selfishness Cure: Empathy (pp. 82-88)

"Rejoice with those who rejoice; mourn with those who mourn." Romans 12:15 (NIV)

1. What is empathy (in your own words)?

2. What are some natural barriers to showing empathy?

3. Why can empathy be so hard at times?

4. Is there something specific you can focus on as a way of reminding yourself to be empathetic toward your spouse (even when it's hard)?

5. What are some practical steps to take to improve your ability to show empathy to your spouse?

Love Languages (pp 88-94)

It's important to recognize that what makes us each feel loved, accepted, and understood is not necessarily the same as what makes our spouse feel that way.

    1. How does that reality affect our ability to show empathy to our spouse?

    2. Have you ever found yourself like Alan, thinking that you are showing love to your spouse by treating him/her the way you would want to be treated?

    3. Can you share an example of how you have found this to be true in your relationship with your spouse (whether positively or negatively)?

One of the ways you can name and change your blind spots is to use Gary Chapman's *The 5 Love Languages* when it comes to how we are loving our spouse.

Those love languages are:

- Words of Affirmation

- Acts of Service

- Receiving Gifts

- Quality Time

- Physical Touch

Spend the remaining time sharing about this as a group using the following questions as a guide.

1. What are each of your respective primary love languages?

2. Are they the same or different for each of you?

3. Is the way you best like to receive love the same or different than the primary way you show love?

4. How does it make you feel when your spouse speaks to you in his/her primary love language rather than your own?

5. How does it make you feel when your spouse speaks to you using your primary love language?

6. Can you share examples of how your spouse does things that speak to you in your primary love language?

If your spouse feels love, acceptance, and understanding from you, that's not only giving them a gift but letting them know you're rooting out selfishness and self-focus in order to love them well.

7. How does showing love to your spouse in his or her primary love language help to do this?

Homework

It's important to find 30 to 60 minutes of uninterrupted time this week to sit down with your spouse and work through the following questions. Pray together at the start and end of your time together, asking God for honesty and grace with each other as you share and for his strength to work on any changes you desire to make.

We believe one way to counteract selfishness and increase empathy toward your spouse is remembering that they are created in the image of God and immensely valuable to him (a beloved son or daughter). Before you get together to spend time to share with them, take some time alone to think about this and then answer the following questions. Be prepared to share your conclusions with your spouse as you are comfortable doing so.

• To what extent are there areas in which you are either selfish or selfless when it comes to your marriage relationship? Ask God to show you areas where you need to become more selfless.

- What specific character traits do I value in my spouse? Does listing these characteristics bring up any new insights for me?

- Discuss each of your primary love languages. Is there a difference in how you naturally give and receive love?

- If there are ways in which your spouse does show love to you in your primary love language, share them with your spouse and affirm him/her for loving you in that way.

- How well have you done at showing your spouse love in his or her primary love language? What specific things can you start to do that expresses love more meaningfully in your spouse's primary love language? If you are comfortable doing so, ask your spouse to share one way you can improve at showing love in his/her primary love language.

Read Chapter 6

Forgiveness

KEY THEME

"Forgiveness can be difficult and is often both a singular-moment decision and a constantly-lived-out-over-years commitment. It takes work and it plays a key role in any effort to build a marriage on purpose."

Chapter 6 - Forgiveness

What Is Forgiveness? (pp. 96-99)

Our definition for the purpose of marriage: no longer holding an offense against our spouse.

A more detailed description: an act of pardoning something that has been done, including giving up resentment, vengefulness, and anger toward someone for an offense, flaw, or mistake he or she has committed.

1. How is forgiveness different than forgetting?

2. Why is this distinction important?

3. Why is forgiveness so important in any relationship, and particularly a marriage?

4. Can you give examples of how seeking and giving forgiveness has changed your marriage?

Five Important Aspects of Forgiveness (pp. 99-106)

Consider what Peter shared about the key aspects of genuine forgiveness:

- Forgiveness is a choice.

- Forgiveness is *not* the same as forgetting.

- Forgiveness is not about the other person deserving it.

- Forgiveness is difficult.

- Don't wait to forgive until you feel like forgiving, because you will never get there.

  1. Which of these five elements is the most convicting or difficult for you? Why?

  2. What do these five aspects tell us about the challenge of truly forgiving someone?

Moving On (pp. 106-110)

Forgiveness is often both a singular-moment decision and a constantly-lived-out-over-years commitment.

1. Discuss how this is true, both with regard to a single act of forgiveness and the fact that we will likely have to forgive our spouse hundreds of times for hundreds of offenses over the course of our marriage.

2. What is Dan's point in showing you this list?

3. Can you give examples of small things that you once disagreed over that now, in hindsight, really did not matter (and that you can now laugh about)?

Homework

It's important to find 30 to 60 minutes of uninterrupted time this week to sit down with your spouse and work through the following questions. Pray together at the start and end of your time together, asking God for honesty and grace with each other as you share and for his strength to work on any changes you desire to make.

NOTE: Before you get together to share, spend some time individually in reflection and prayer asking God to reveal areas in your own life where you either need to forgive your spouse (whether or not they ask for forgiveness) or there are things you have done that you need to seek forgiveness from your spouse.

- Do you struggle with seeking forgiveness for things you have done to wrong or hurt your spouse? What makes it so difficult for you?

- Is forgiving another person normally easy or difficult for you? Why? Which of the five aspects of genuine forgiveness normally is the most difficult for you? Why?

- If you are comfortable and ready to do so, seek forgiveness for the things God has brought to mind as you reflected and prayed about things this week. Similarly, if there are areas where you have forgiven your spouse, share about that forgiveness.

Read Chapter 7

Apologizing

KEY THEME

"...learning how to genuinely apologize and then actually
doing it is yet another key to a great relationship."

Chapter 7 - Apologizing

Apologizing and Repentance (pp. 111-113)

In this chapter we compare apologizing to repentance (to change your mind, turn around, or course correct).

1. How does this comparison help us to understand what genuinely apologizing involves?

2. What is the primary purpose of apologizing to someone we have hurt (whether intentionally or not)?

3. Is apologizing the same thing as asking for forgiveness? Why or why not?

The Seven Key Aspects of Genuine Apology (pp. 113-119)

We have identified seven key aspects of any genuine apology:

1. Admit what you did.

2. Check your body language and tone.

3. Genuinely apologize.

4. Do something different next time.

5. Determine what went wrong.

6. Keep the goal in mind.

7. Live it out.

1. Which of these seven aspects is the most convicting or difficult for you? Why?

2. In light of these points, how hard is it for you to genuinely apologize?

3. Can you share a personal example about how a genuine apology or request for forgiveness made a positive difference in your marriage?

Homework

It's important to find 30 to 60 minutes of uninterrupted time this week to sit down with your spouse and work through the following questions. Pray together at the start and end of your time together, asking God for honesty and grace with each other as you share and for his strength to work on any changes you desire to make.

NOTE: Before you get together to share, spend some time individually in reflection and prayer asking God to reveal areas in your own life where you need to apologize.

- Do you struggle with apologizing for things you have done to wrong or hurt your spouse? What makes it so difficult for you? Are there any of the areas of genuinely apologizing that you need to improve on?

- If you are comfortable and ready to do so, apologize to your spouse for the things God has brought to mind as you reflected and prayed about things this week.

Read Chapter 8

Differences

KEY THEME

"Problems aren't caused by differences. They're caused by not handling differences well. The key is to handle them in a way that makes you both feel valued, heard, and understood."

Chapter 8 - Differences

The Challenge (pp. 121-125)

The journey of marriage is about growing in accepting our spouse instead of changing them (or getting our way), which is too often our goal when expressing a frustration.

1. What are some areas where you and your spouse have differences of opinion?

2. In the grand scheme of life, how important are the issues where you have differences?

As you think about all of this, remember the 90/10 Rule and the importance of recognizing that you share at least 10% of the need to change and take responsibility when things go wrong or are difficult.

3. How does this suggestion help with managing differences of opinion?

Irreconcilable Differences (pp. 125-130)

Anytime we refuse to compromise and desperately hold on to our need to have our preference acknowledged as "right," we can find ourselves in the middle of an "irreconcilable difference." We believe this is normal, and that our way forward in a purposeful marriage is through compromise (consistently, and from both sides).

1. Can you share examples of where you and your spouse have faced "irreconcilable differences" over what could ultimately be relatively minor or personal preference issues?

2. How did you move past them?

3. Are there some that remain irreconcilable? If so, how do you handle that?

We understand that as the stakes of a decision rise higher and higher, the need for grace, kindness, and clear communication continues. Short of situations requiring coaching or counseling, we suggest that the solution involves choosing kindness and compromise (instead of holding on to the need to be right), which requires sacrifice and surrender.

4. Can you share examples of where you and your spouse have faced "irreconcilable differences" over what were more serious or fundamental issues?

5. How did you move past them?

6. Are there some that remain irreconcilable? If so, how do you handle that?

Homework

It's important to find 30 to 60 minutes of uninterrupted time this week to sit down with your spouse and work through the following questions. Pray together at the start and end of your time together, asking God for honesty and grace with each other as you share and for his strength to work on any changes you desire to make.

NOTE: Before you get together to share, spend some time individually in reflection and prayer asking God to reveal areas in your marriage where you have differences of opinion. Go through that list and identify those which are more minor (e.g., personal preference) and which are more serious. Ask God to show you where you have ownership in the difference of opinion, where you can simply let go of more minor things, and where and how you can show kindness and compromise in more serious matters.

- Discuss the areas where you and your spouse have differences of opinion. Which of them are more minor (matters of personal preference) and which are more serious?

- For the areas that are more minor, discuss how each of you might compromise or defer to your spouse on matters of personal preference. For areas that are more serious, discuss where each of you might compromise. Or, if you can't come up with a compromise, whether you are both open to counseling or coaching to help you get through it.

Read Chapter 9

Staying Connected

KEY THEME

"Three keys to stay connected and fight the natural tendency to drift apart are spending time together, having common goals, and tapping into your marriage reserve tank."

Chapter 9 - Staying Connected

Spend Time Together (pp. 131-137)

Spending consistent time together, especially doing things you both enjoy, will help keep you from drifting apart.

1. Why is spending time together so important and what does making it a priority say to our spouse?

2. What kinds of things do you and your spouse do together to stay connected? Were these natural or things that you had to work hard at?

3. If this was hard and you had to work at it, what helped you to be successful?

Set Goals Together (pp. 137-138)

The key to goal setting is to be intentional about setting aside time for these talks and both of you knowing what the conversation will be about.

1. Why are conversations about shared goals essential in avoiding drift in your relationship?

2. How successful have you and your spouse been at having discussions about common goals and then working together to achieve them?

3. What are some hindrances that make this hard? What are some keys to making it work?

4. Can you share a story about how you successfully set and achieved a goal in your marriage?

Tap into Your Marriage Reserve Tank (pp. 139-142)

When we face the inevitable tough or difficult times in our marriage, we need to rely on our reserve tank filled with memories of better times – times when we overcame difficulties together or where we clearly saw God at work in our lives.

1. Have you ever faced one of those points in your marriage where you wondered whether it was a mistake or whether you should or could stick it out?

2. How did you move past it? Did you find it helpful to tap into your marriage reserve tank of positive memories?

We talk about how perseverance or "grit" is a big part of a great marriage.

3. Can you share an experience in which you or your spouse (or both) showed real "grit" to keep your marriage going through a tough time?

4. How does that experience give you confidence for the future of your marriage?

Homework

It's important to find 30 to 60 minutes of uninterrupted time this week to sit down with your spouse and work through the following questions. Pray together at the start and end of your time together, asking God for honesty and grace with each other as you share and for his strength to work on any changes you desire to make.

Share the things that you do together to stay connected that are most meaningful to you. Is there something new either of you would like to try together that you can share?

- How purposeful are you about goal setting for your marriage? Are there one or two key goals you both want to focus on in the next few weeks to help deepen and strengthen your marriage?

- Reflect with your spouse on your marriage and talk about where you faced tough times that you overcame together or where God showed up to help. Make a list of them (your "reserve tank").

- How is your "reserve tank" list helpful to you today? Keep this list someplace safe so you can reference it and tap into it the next time things get difficult.

A Closing Note from the Authors:

We hope that this discussion guide helped you take a deeper, and more personal, look at the topics that we addressed in *Marriage on Purpose*. As hard as it can be to share openly in a group or one-on-one setting, the benefits far outweigh the discomfort that comes along with being vulnerable. We have each found that to be true in our own lives and we trust that you've found that to be the case as you've gone through this study guide. It's important to remember that our relationships can't grow and we can't grow individually unless we identify growth opportunities and actively work to do something different than what we've done in the past.

Please don't close this workbook and check it off your list as "done." Working on your marriage is an ongoing process, and the need for growth will continue for the duration of your relationship. That's true for everybody. Whether you're newlyweds or a couple who's been married for 70 years, nobody has "arrived" and gotten to a point of no longer needing to grow, surrender, and forgive. We pray that *Marriage on Purpose* and this study guide have been encouraging and challenging for you along the journey.

Dan, Peter, and Alan

STRATEGIES FOR
GROWING YOUR MARRIAGE

10 Tips for Praying with Your Spouse

As we wrote about in Chapter 1, praying with your spouse is an absolutely vital part of making God the foundation of any marriage. With that in mind, here are some helpful tips to get started:

1. Make praying together a priority. Set a reminder on your phone to help you make time until it becomes a habit.

2. Pick a time of day that works best for success. If you pray together in the evening, be mindful of the time so you're not too tired and drift off to sleep.

3. Find a place where you can pray without interruption.

4. When you first start out, focus your prayer time together on your marriage and on each person's individual needs.

5. Take turns praying. If one of you is more comfortable than the other, have that person start. Then the other person can join in or say his or her own prayer.

6. If you're having a really hard time getting started, try a conversational prayer where you just talk to each other about your needs and then close by asking for God's help.

7. Start with short prayers until you get used to praying together.

8. Write out some of the things you want to remember to pray about. It's okay to pray with your eyes open so you can look at your notes.

9. As a way to remind yourselves to stay connected, hold hands or embrace while you pray. Remember that prayer is simply talking to God.

10. You don't have to use big theological terms or sound "spiritual." Just pour out your heart to God. He's the only one who can really help.

Top Three Takeaways

1.

2.

3.

Additional Notes:

Goals for Your Marriage

Individual Goals

   1.

   2.

   3.

Couple Goals

   1.

   2.

   3.

Winning At Home encourages people at
all ages and stages of family development
to lead Christ-centered homes.

OTHER TITLES FROM WINNING AT HOME

All titles are available at
winningathome.com

**Once-A-Day: Nurturing
Great Kids Devotional**
*365 Practical Insights for
Parenting with Grace*

By Dan Seaborn

The Necessary Nine
How to Stay Happily Married for Life!

By Dan Seaborn &
Dr. Peter Newhouse
with Lisa Velthouse

Journeying with Pain
*Finding Hope When You
Don't Find Answers*

By Alan Seaborn

Winning the Battle Over Abuse
A Self-Directed Guide to Healing

By Dr. Peter Newhouse

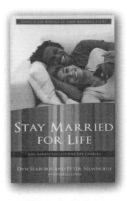

One-Minute Reflections for Couples:
Marriage Rendezvous, Stay Married for Life, Two to One, Leaving a Legacy

By Dan Seaborn & Dr. Peter Newhouse with Susan Lewis

Marriage: Five Years Later
Lessons From the Early Years

By Alan Seaborn

Prescriptions for Healthy Relationships

By Dr. Peter Newhouse

SUPPORTING MARRIAGES & FAMILIES THROUGH

Counseling Services

Our staff of licensed professionals counsel individuals, couples, and families, helping them to overcome barriers and develop toward wholeness. We offer counseling for married couples, premarital couples, single parents, adoptive and blended families, divorce recovery, mood disorders, communication issues, domestic violence situations, and so much more. We have counselors who work with adults as well as children and adolescents.

Coaching Services

We have a team of certified coaches who can provide the guidance you need when you get stuck in a certain area of your life or relationships or you just need help pushing forward in meeting goals or clarifying your purpose in life. We provide individual and marriage coaching, group or team coaching, as well as corporate and leadership coaching.

Community Events

Community events are a unique opportunity for us to combine the strength of community with the joy of relationships. Whether to support our mission or strengthen bonds of trust and love in relationships, our events are done in creative and fun ways that make the information easy to receive, retain, and carry through in relationships.

Speakers

Our speakers strive to bring a message of love, hope, peace, and unity to individuals, marriages, and families through whatever topic is addressed. Their goal is to motivate audiences to thought, reflection, and often action, as needed, to help participants achieve their ultimate desired outcomes or reach some helpful conclusions to move forward.

Winning At Home